BACK ROADS

PEOPLE, PLACES AND PIE AROUND VIRGINIA

Text by Bill Lohmann

Photos by Bob Brown

Richmond Times-Dispatch

TimesDispatch.com

Foreword

You're holding in your hands a warm and glowing slice of life: a joyous collaboration that gives us Virginians much for which to be thankful and grateful. Most of you know these two seasoned observers. Not just for their distinguished journalistic contributions, but for all the recent ramblings in the *Richmond Times-Dispatch* along Routes 58 and 11, filling our eyes and hearts with glimpses of life in our commonwealth today and how they connect us to simpler, less hurried and often yearned-for yesterdays. *Back Roads: People, Places and Pie Around Virginia* adds substantially to the impressive Brown-Lohmann collection of masterful duets.

Bob brings his experience, his patience and his eye to the art of capturing images that seem too perfectly lit and composed to be Photoshop-free. And he obviously takes great joy in his freedom from the constraints of his decades stalking politicos at the State Capitol. And Bill is a writer with the heart of our favorite uncle with a deep and abiding appreciation of the things that make life worth living. I won't open an argument about how many words a picture is worth — this keepsake volume simply strikes the perfect balance between the two.

To borrow the old Candid Camera line, this is Virginia caught in the act of being herself, and in the process, reminding us why we love calling this place home. We just couldn't have asked for two better guys to pool their talents to our advantage. This book gives us the reassurance that things we feared might be lost are still very much with us.

Tim Timberlake
August 2013

Table of Contents

Introduction

I arrived at The Richmond News Leader in 1988 and hadn't worked there too long when I noticed this photographer hanging around reporters' desks, chatting them up and suggesting ideas for stories. Soon enough, he started coming around to see me once in a while, and he often arrived with a recommendation for a piece that he thought might get a good ride in the paper and, oh, by the way, he'd be glad to shoot it.

I bit on a few of these — after all, they were good story ideas — and that's how I came to know Bob Brown. After a while it dawned on me that we shared a common goal: to stay out of the office as much as possible. And what better way to do that than to venture into the fresh air chasing worthy stories?

It didn't hurt that Bob is the perfect colleague: great at his job, enthusiastic about the work and easy to get along with. We also both like pie and gravy. Over the years, we've covered many kinds of stories together — from presidential inaugurations to food festivals — and we've carved out a nice little niche reporting on people and places around Virginia.

In 2002, we produced story-and-picture packages every week for six months on U.S. 58, the longest road in Virginia. We followed that with "10 Places You Need To See In Virginia" as well as "Back Roads," an occasional series of stories from out-of-the-way places around the commonwealth.

The mistaken impression about our traveling is that we are on the road constantly. In reality, we travel only occasionally, though we do try to come home with a fistful of stories from every trip. When you add up the years, we've certainly logged a lot of miles together. We always have fun, and in all that time I can't remember a cross word between us. That might be because I'm deaf in one ear so I hear only about half of what he says, and I ignore the rest.

I like reminding Bob that we started in the newspaper business at about the same time. Of course, he was a staff photographer with almost a decade of experience in the television business, and I was a 5th-grader delivering papers from my bicycle. Those are the times he ignores me.

Bill Lohmann
August 2013

ABOVE: Bill Lohmann, actor Robert Duvall and Bob Brown. PHOTO BY LUCIANA DUVALL

■ In front of his Hard Times Antiques in Stickleyville in 2002, Steven Taylor talked about being laid off from his mining job. He sold, as you can see, a little of everything.

PEOPLE

Friends

Readers often ask, "How do you find these people you write about?"

Like this:

We were sitting at the counter in the Hillsville Diner on a Saturday morning in 2002, gathering material — and eating breakfast, of course — for a story in our series on U.S. 58. We were chatting with the amiable owner, Mac McPeak, when the door opened and in walked an older gentleman who looked to be maybe 70 and, based on the reception he received from other customers, was clearly a regular.

"Here's the man you ought to be writing about!" McPeak told us.

We asked, in so many words and in the nicest way possible, why is that? Many people offer us story suggestions, and while everyone certainly has a story, some stories, we have discovered, are better

than others. We tried to hide our skepticism as we worked on our eggs and bacon.

"Wilford operates a diesel shovel at the quarry down the road!" McPeak said with enthusiasm.

We sort of said, "OK."

"He works five days a week, and he leaves home at 4 o'clock every morning!" McPeak said.

We sort of said, "OK."

"Wilford's my first customer every week-day morning!" McPeak said. "I don't open until 5, but I let him in early!"

We sort of said, "OK," and, not having heard anything that sounded like the next great story, were trying to think of a way to gracefully change the direction of the conversation without hurting anyone's feelings.

McPeak is a nice, patient man, but you could see he was growing frustrated with us.

"Well," McPeak finally said, exasperated with us, "he is 90 years old!"

"Why didn't you say so!" we replied.

So, we met Walter Wilford Burnette, who, it turns out, helped dig the foundation for the Pentagon, worked on the Blue Ridge Parkway, loaded rock used in construction of the Chesapeake Bay Bridge-Tunnel and churned through swamps to dig highways and a canal on property that would become Walt Disney World.

And we left the diner with another story.

ABOVE: As a chilly dawn broke in December 2002, Walter Wilford Burnette, who turned 91 by the time we wrote about him, arrived at his job at a quarry near Hillsville. He operated the diesel shovel in the background.

ABOVE: Donna Rohrer, an Old Order Mennonite, paused from weeding a vegetable garden on a Rockingham County farm to speak with a visitor in 2008.

LEFT AND BELOW LEFT: Nationally known comedian Brett Leake, who is able to poke fun at his disability and describes himself as a "sit-down, stand-up comic," provided care and companionship for his father, Francis Leake, at their home in Louisa County. Both men were diagnosed with a form of muscular dystrophy. In a June 2008 interview, Francis Leake emotionally described how the most routine of tasks in earlier years had become impossible for him as the disease progressed. Francis Leake died in January 2009.

ABOVE RIGHT: Ira Wallace displayed products offered by the Southern Exposure Seed Exchange in Louisa County in 2010.

LEFT: Wilson Jessee, an 88-year-old tobacco farmer in Russell County, was tending to his hilltop crop near Castlewood in September 2003.

ABOVE: Morton Adelanski was a signature Richmond character who was born deaf but never let that slow him down, as he traveled around the city and the country, sometimes hitchhiking as he did here on Monument Avenue in 1995. Adelanski worked for a Richmond florist, sold ice cream and other snacks at sporting events and was a friend to governors and anyone else he encountered.

RIGHT: Ida and Anthony Trigiani, at their home in Big Stone Gap in September 2002, raised seven children, including daughter Adriana, who often writes of life in Southwest Virginia.

BELOW: Amy Ladd (left) and Judie Balacke entertained Richmond radio listeners in 2008 on their "Sunday Morning Gospel" show.

ABOVE: On a cold day in January 2012, music legend Ralph Stanley, a son of Southwest Virginia, visited the family cemetery in Dickenson County where he will be buried.

LEFT: Randall L. 'Scooty' Lillard, a Madison County farmer and longtime chief election officer in Graves Mill, kept watch on the antique boxes where the precinct's 70 registered voters still placed their paper ballots in 2000.

RIGHT: Historical interpreters James Price and Stephanie Murray, both of Afton, were at work in October 2007 on the Mountain Trail Farm near Humpback Rocks on the Blue Ridge Parkway.

BELOW RIGHT: In 2008, Connie Stevens worked behind the counter at the House of Deals in Onancock on Virginia's Eastern Shore.

ABOVE: At his shop in 2005, Wayne Henderson, a retired letter carrier born and raised in the small community of Rugby in Grayson County, has become an internationally respected guitarist and guitar-maker. He's also a heck of a nice guy.

RIGHT: Steven G. Meeks, president of the Albemarle Charlottesville Historical Society, watched over the historic Hatton Ferry on the James River near Scottsville in July 2010.

LEFT: Staunton's Willy Ferguson, known for his large metal sculptures, explained in 2010 how this large sphere worked as a sundial.

BELOW LEFT: Civic booster Mary Woodruff posed with one of the murals painted on buildings in Emporia in 2010 in an effort to spruce up downtown.

ABOVE AND LEFT: E. Bruce Heilman, 82 in these 2008 photos, is a World War II Marine and retired president of the University of Richmond, who has become a role model for those who wish to remain active in their later years by taking long road trips on his Harley-Davidson motorcycle.

TOP LEFT: Dr. Richard L. Hoffman, curator of recent invertebrates at the Virginia Museum of Natural History in Martinsville, showed us a jar of Virginia tarantulas on a 2002 visit.

TOP MIDDLE: Thomas Dodson rocked the foundation of the Clifton Primitive Baptist Church in Fairfax County during the Historic Clifton Candlelight Tour in December 2004.

TOP RIGHT: Mike Puffenbarger watched the sap drip into one of his maple syrup buckets in Highland County in February 2004.

RIGHT: Glennadine Gouldman, of Gum Springs, district director of Motor Maids, a national women's motorcycle organization, said in an interview for a 2003 story on Harley-Davidson's 100th anniversary that she was known as "Grandma Harley."

BELOW: A migrant laborer who rode for three days with a bus full of other workers from Laredo, Texas, arrived in South Boston in June 2002, where he and the others were met by local farmers needing help in their fields.

TOP: Calvin R. Crane, 96, son of a Confederate veteran from the Civil War, posed in April 2013 with a Confederate battle flag he flew on special occasions at his home in Roanoke.

ABOVE: Isabelle Hammock Hodges, 88, looked over the pile of cards she has received from well-wishers since word got out that she was a "real daughter" of a Confederate soldier. She was interviewed in April 2013 at her home near Rocky Mount.

LEFT: Bobby Street, farm manager for the Lost World Ranch in Burke's Garden, nuzzled one of the farm's camels in 2007.

ABOVE: Rastus Hatley, who at age 86 said he still worked the peach orchards near Broadnax, had stopped by Whitby's Orchard and Produce Country Store in June 2002.

RIGHT: Christina King, 16, followed by brother, Jack, 11, and other King children, bounded down the stairs of their Eastern Shore home in November 2007. Mike and Meg King adopted 20 children, mostly from Russia.

BELOW: Sharon Sun Eagle, with Riley, talked about how her brother-in-law needed a new trailer, among other things, on the Mattaponi Reservation in November 2009. From her home on the reservation, Sun Eagle operated a grassroots charity, Spirit Rising, to benefit Native Americans in Virginia and elsewhere around the United States.

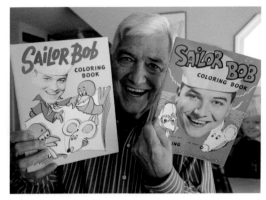

ABOVE: To a generation of children in Richmond and throughout the countryside of Central Virginia, Bob Griggs always will be "Sailor Bob," the amiable and artistic host of a popular television show that aired from the late 1950s until the 1970s. Griggs was photographed at his Chesterfield County home in October 2010.

LEFT: Lisa Dearden with Cupcake, one of her favorite chickens, on her small farm in Goochland County in 2013.

BELOW: Glendi Garfield 'Sug' Branscome, age 100 (center), shared a laugh with his youngest son, Donnie (right) and friend Howard Shrewbury, over breakfast in August 2006 at the Hillsville Diner.

Robert Duvall

On the morning we were to interview actor Robert Duvall at his farm in Fauquier County, we left Richmond a few minutes early so we could stop in Warranton at the Red Truck Bakery.

Bakeries are not unusual places for us to visit, but we had a particular mission at Red Truck: In reading up on Duvall in advance of the interview, I'd learned he occasionally showed up at Red Truck to hang out with locals. The bakery even sold something called "Bobby's Breakfast in a Box," a collection of coffee cake, bread, coffee and homemade granola that Duvall and his wife, Luciana, like to send as gifts.

We asked Red Truck owner Brian Noyes what kind of pie the Duvalls enjoyed and he replied, "Apple." The purchase of one apple pie later, we were back on the road. We are not above using baked goods to enhance an interview.

We drove up the appropriately long drive of the Duvalls' 360-acre farm, and Luciana greeted us at the front door. We handed her the pie. A few minutes later, Duvall strode into the living room, smiled, shook our hands and started talking. "What's up! Good to see you! Bobby Duvall! How are you?"

We were fine.

One of the great actors of our time then launched into a very down-to-earth description of the magical work of an elephant named Bubbles who had visited the Duvalls' place a few months earlier during a charity event for the Robert Duvall Children's Fund. During her stay, Bubbles had resided in a field where the Duvalls now were harvesting a bumper crop of fabulous pumpkins.

"I don't know much about elephants," Duvall said with the sort of enthusiasm one might use in offering a positive assessment of a nuclear physicist or a plumber who fixed a leaky faucet, "but she was terrific!"

Duvall's publicist had promised us 15 minutes; Duvall gave us every bit of two hours, driving us around his property, showing us a barn he'd refurbished for entertaining — with, among other touches, a saloon-style bar that would have fit right onto the set of "Lonesome Dove" — and, of course, the pumpkin patch.

ABOVE AND OPPOSITE TOP: Academy Award-winning actor Robert Duvall chatted about acting, soccer and elephants, among other topics, in the living room of his Fauquier County home in September 2011.

BELOW: Duvall and his wife, Luciana, proudly showed off the bumper crop of pumpkins at their estate.

Lee County Predators

We stopped for a late lunch at a place called Rooster's Pub in Pennington Gap, in the far southwest corner of Virginia.

We finished our sandwiches, and Bob, his ever-present Leica hanging from his neck, struck up a conversation with our young waitress. In time, the talk turned to what we were up to — gathering material along U.S. 58 for our 2002 Virginia Beach-to-Cumberland Gap series — and he explained we were looking around Lee County for things to include in our stories.

"You should write about our football team!" she said.

Bob told her we did indeed plan to return in the fall and attend a game at Lee County High School, Friday nights watching the Generals being a big social event in the rural community.

"No," she said, "I meant our football team."

We soon learned about the Lee County Predators, a women's amateur, full-contact football team that played women's teams from the area, including just over the border in Tennessee and Kentucky. We further learned our waitress, Amanda Goins, a mother of two, was the quarterback.

"I was nervous before the first game," she told us later. "But once I got hit a few times, I was fine, and I haven't been nervous since."

So, we returned not only in the fall to catch the boys' high school team but the following spring to cover a Predators game. The Predators came from all walks of life: a florist, a nurse, a school teacher. A few sported tattoos, some wore mascara behind their facemasks and at least three rode Harleys.

The star running back, a college student, had to miss the game because she promised her boyfriend she would go to his high school prom with him. So, she showed up just before the game, in a lovely gown, to wish her teammates well.

"This is killing me," she said of not being able to play against the Tennessee Mountain Catz.

The hitting was ferocious on both sides, but a little more ferocious by the Mountain Catz, who came away with a 40-0 victory.

But at the Predators' post-game party at Rooster's Pub it was difficult to tell who lost: the beer was cold, the laughter loud, the camaraderie stronger than ever.

I wondered what the scene would have been like had the Predators actually won.

Said school principal and defensive tackle Connie Daugherty, "Exactly like this."

OPPOSITE: All dressed up, Anya Hobbs, the star running back for the Lee County Predators, stopped by to wish her teammates well before their game in May 2003 against the Tennessee Mountain Catz. Hobbs was on her way to the Lee County High prom.

ABOVE: Aimee Jones, a defensive end and offensive guard for the Predators, eyed the action from behind her facemask.

LEFT: Quarterback Amanda Goins, and her biggest fans: children 1-year-old Ashton and 2-year-old Devin.

BELOW: Predators defensive tackle Connie Daugherty chased a Tennessee running back.

Thomas Cannon

Thomas Cannon liked being known as "the poor man's philanthropist."

Over three decades, he gave away more than $150,000, mostly to strangers and usually in the form of $1,000 checks, on his modest salary from the U.S. Postal Service. He was a singular character who lived frugally, wrote eloquently and laughed loudly. He was humble but outspoken, and generally kept a low profile though he didn't mind the occasional national television interview.

As a result of their uncommon generosity to others, he and his wife, Princetta, lived for many years in a rundown home in a neighborhood that might be considered the back roads of Richmond. Admirers eventually purchased a house near Maymont for the Cannons when word got out that Princetta was bedridden from strokes and Tom was providing round-the-clock care. She died in 2000.

Tom Cannon traced his benevolence to his time in the Navy during World War II when an explosion on his former ship killed several friends after he had been sent to gunnery school. He wondered why he'd been spared, finally coming to believe that his mission on earth was to assist those in need.

He often gave money to people he read about in the Richmond newspapers, but rarely met them, usually sending the checks to reporters who had written the stories and asking them to make the happy deliveries.

I delivered a few of those checks, and Bob photographed Cannon from time to time. In 2004, when Cannon was 78, we took him on a road trip to Chase City, the small Southside Virginia town where he grew up with his mother, three siblings and grandmother in a three-room shack that had neither electricity nor running water. Despite the hardships, he called them "the happiest days of my life."

The next year, we visited Cannon again, but this time the occasion was far more somber: he had been diagnosed with inoperable cancer, and his days were numbered — except he wasn't somber at all. He asked if we'd bring him lunch, so we sat around eating cheeseburgers and listening to the 25-minute funeral tape — for his funeral — that he had produced, not trusting anyone else to get it just right. He called it his "Bon Voyage Program."

"I have no fear of death," said Cannon, a few months before he died in 2005. It was his final mission to make others feel more comfortable about their mortality, and it was, in a way, his final gift.

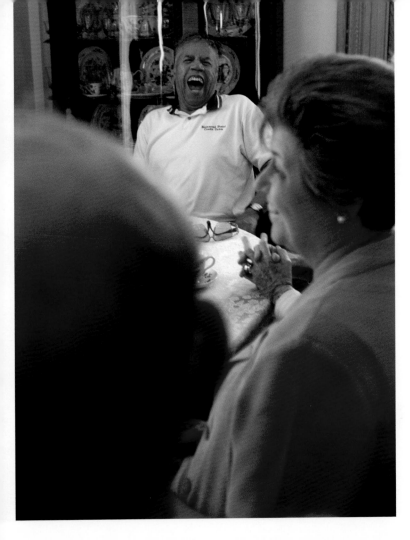

LEFT: Thomas Cannon kept the laughter rolling during a luncheon in his honor in Chase City in June 2004. The event was attended by community leaders including Chase City Industrial Development Association chairman Charles Duckworth (left) and his wife, Bettie Duckworth, who was in charge of the Business Education Partnership for Mecklenburg County.

OPPOSITE: The demonstrative Cannon, in his Richmond home in 1995, as he cared for his bedridden wife, Princetta.

BOTTOM LEFT: Cannon cracks up his childhood friend, W.T. "Thad" Carter, who was driving him around his old neighborhood in Chase City in June 2004.

BOTTOM RIGHT: In May 2005, Cannon sat in his living room, intently listening to the service he had recorded for his funeral.

Chief Justice

Here's a bit of advice if you ever find yourself in an all-terrain vehicle with the first female chief justice of the Virginia Supreme Court at the wheel:

Hang on tight.

She's not a bad driver or anything, but ATVs being what they are you really don't want to be bounced out of the vehicle as you're riding with a judge through the fields to check on a herd of heifers. It might be embarrassing.

Chief Justice Cynthia Dinah Fannon Kinser generously welcomed us to her home in Pennington Gap in late 2010 in advance of her investiture as Virginia's 25th chief justice. We arrived in Lee County, the westernmost corner of Virginia, late in the afternoon, following a brief autumn cloudburst that left the air clear and the landscape dazzling.

Besides giving us the aforementioned tour of her family farm aboard an ATV — an exercise she finds "relaxing" after a day of reading briefs and writing opinions — Kinser and husband, Allen, met us for dinner at a favorite Mexican restaurant. She also took us to her mother's house to meet her mom, Velda Fannon, and her brother, Sid, and they served us pumpkin pie, topped with whipped cream.

Kinser is a true daughter of Southwest Virginia, having spent most of her life in Pennington Gap. The Kentucky line is less than 10 miles from the center of town.

In school, the low-key Kinser played clarinet and performed as a majorette, but her most influential activity was the 4-H youth organization, for which she raised steers, researched nutrition and developed leadership and speaking skills. As a high

school senior, she won a trip to a 4-H conference in Chicago. It was her first airplane ride. She went away to college — she graduated from the University of Tennessee and the University of Virginia School of Law — but she returned to Southwest Virginia to live. When we talked to her, she still regularly played pipe organ at First United Methodist Church.

"It gives you a sense of belonging," she said of her deep roots in the community. "I grew up knowing my grandparents. There's something to be said for that. Not everybody can do that … but it was possible for us to do. We never really seriously thought about living anyplace else."

LEFT: Virginia Supreme Court Justice Cynthia Kinser flips through a hymnal inside the First United Methodist Church at Pennington Gap where she occasionally served as organist.

OPPOSITE: Kinser checked on cattle at her family farm in Lee County in November 2010.

BOTTOM LEFT: Kinser played piano for residents of the Lee Nursing and Rehabilitation Center in Pennington Gap.

BOTTOM RIGHT: Kinser and her husband, Allen, chatted over dinner at El Centenario, a favorite restaurant of theirs in Pennington Gap.

TOP LEFT: Velda Fannon, the chief justice's mother, greeted visitors to her home with a piece of pie.

TOP RIGHT: In her office at Pennington Gap, Kinser talked about growing up in Southwest Virginia.

RIGHT: Kinser rehearsed a hymn at First United Methodist Church in Pennington Gap.

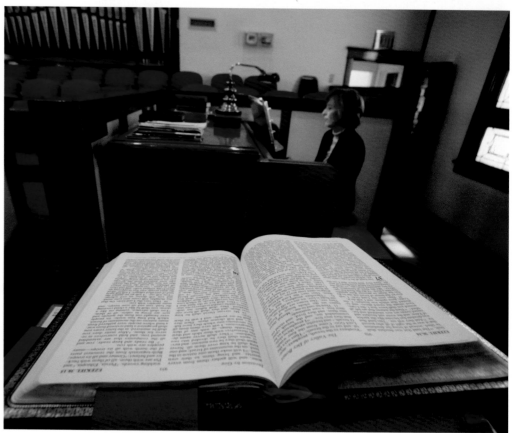

LEFT: In her chambers in Richmond, Kinser slipped on her judicial robe, preparing for a court session in November 2010.

BELOW: As Justice Donald W. Lemons listened, Kinser spoke to the Supreme Court after being sworn in as chief justice in February 2011.

Ralph Stanley

Bob has known Ralph Stanley for years, having photographed him for several stories, including in 2001 when he rode along with the Clinch Mountain Boys to the Grand Ole Opry. I'd never met Stanley until a cold day in January 2012 when we visited his home on Doctor Ralph Stanley Highway deep in the mountains of Southwest Virginia. He'd been nominated for another Grammy award.

Stanley was about to turn 85, but he was still going strong, playing gigs in venues ranging from the Opry to Ruritan Clubs and all in between, and living the life of a musical icon. How else would you describe a man who lives on a road that bears his name, had been officially proclaimed a "Living Legend" by the Library of Congress and could lead you on a tour of his own museum? As he showed us around the Ralph Stanley Museum and Traditional Mountain Music Center in Clintwood, he even treated us to a few verses of "O Death," the haunting song that helped introduce him and his distinctive voice to a new generation of fans in the 2000 film "O Brother, Where Art Thou?"

"The icing on the cake," Stanley said of the acclaim the movie brought him.

Stanley was born and raised in the rugged beauty of Dickenson County, and resisted the pull of Nashville. A shy, quiet man of great loyalty, Stanley said he figured he could get wherever he needed from the roads of Southwest Virginia. We interviewed him in the same house near Coeburn that he and wife Jimmi had shared since 1973. His tour bus was parked out back.

As we followed Stanley over and through the mountains to Clintwood, we stopped at his old home place in McClure. The wind whipped, and the steel-gray sky spit sleet as he walked us to a ridge with a sweeping view. There, we found the family cemetery and Stanley's final resting place: his marker already is etched with his name and a banjo.

"I know one of these days I won't be around," he told us, "but I'll never completely retire until I have to."

ABOVE: A contemplative Ralph Stanley in the living room of his home outside Coeburn in January 2012.

TOP LEFT: Stanley was born and raised in Dickenson County where he still lived at the time of the 2012 interview.

TOP RIGHT: The Grammy Award Stanley won for "O Death," on display at the Ralph Stanley Museum and Traditional Mountain Music Center in Clintwood.

LEFT: Stanley led the Clinch Mountain Boys as they performed at the Grand Ole Opry in Nashville, Tenn., in 2001.

BELOW: Before leaving home to give visitors a tour of the place where he grew up, Stanley gave wife, Jimmi, a kiss.

VMI Women

Charming in its own distinctive way, Virginia Military Institute, which instills a rare kind of loyalty in those who survive it, always has been a source of good stories over the years. The school is not for everyone — and even many who wind up graduating think at one time or other it isn't for them either — nor does it claim to be. Those who make it through VMI say they feel well-prepared for whatever might follow in life.

The battle over admitting women to the school was a dramatic period in VMI history. I covered the original 1991 trial in federal court in Roanoke at which VMI successfully defended its men-only admissions policy. Five years later, the U.S. Supreme Court ruled against the school, and the first young women were enrolled in 1997. Bob covered their arrival in Lexington.

We returned to VMI in 2007 on the 10th anniversary of the arrival of women, visiting with students and administrators, and we also talked to members of that first class of female cadets, wondering how they viewed the experience a decade later. It was interesting to see how much things at VMI had changed following the arrival of women — and how much they hadn't.

One thing we noticed that was no different was the love-hate relationship that men long had expressed about VMI: can't wait to leave it and then when they leave they can't wait to get back.

"I was one of those people who said, 'I will never come back here. I hate this place. This place has been nothing but bad things for me,'" said Kelly Sullivan, a member of the first class of women at VMI who graduated in 2001. "Then I realized, it was nothing but good things for me."

ABOVE: In April 2001, a month before graduation, the 13 remaining women from the original 30 who started at Virginia Military Institute in the first class that included female cadets. The group included (left to right): Kelly K. Sullivan, Melissa S. Williams, Maria M. Vasile, Alexis Abrams, Tamina M. Mars, Jennifer N. Boensch, Kimberly H. Herbert, Erin N. Claunch, Kendra L. Russell, Megan K. Smith, Tennille Chisholm, Angela L. Winters and Rachel Love.

ABOVE: A class ring belonging to a first-classman, or senior, rests on the table inside the barracks at VMI in Lexington.

LEFT: A female cadet lines up with other members of her company in 2001.

BELOW: Members of the VMI cadre marched into the barracks courtyard Wednesday in August 1997 as members of the freshman class, or "rats," the first to include female cadets, line the sides. The famed "rat line" began moments later when the cadre rushed among the freshmen and began barking orders.

ABOVE: Roxanne M. Franck, of Poquoson, marched with her company to the mess hall at VMI in April 2007.

RIGHT: Kim Herbert, a member of the first class of women admitted to VMI in 1997, talked about her experiences at VMI a decade later during a June 2007 lunch meeting at a restaurant in Washington, D.C.

BELOW: Herbert (center) received instruction from a member of the VMI cadre in August 1997 during an early-morning physical-training session. Years earlier, Herbert's brother had attended VMI, but he died in a car crash during his freshman year.

ABOVE: Footware belonging to Jennifer N. Boensch, one of the original female cadets at VMI, inside her barracks room in April 2001.

LEFT: Cadet Becky Harris marched in a parade at VMI in April 2007.

BELOW: VMI freshmen Asia T. Pastor (left) and Sarah L. McIntosh (center) helped prepare senior Mira A. Veis for a parade in April 2007.

■ Bill Shelburne, a retired school teacher, farmer and life-long resident of Dot, held up a mirror in August 2002 to show the signs for entering and leaving the tiny crossroads community in Lee County were on the same post.

PLACES

Going Places

When we embarked on our U.S. 58 se-ries in 2002, we made a list of places we definitely wanted to include. Dot was one of those places, which was something of a leap of faith because neither Bob nor I had ever seen Dot. We knew it only from a map — a speck about 50 miles west of Bristol, on the way to Cumberland Gap — but had a feeling any place called "Dot" had to be worth a stop.

It was, though it wasn't quite what we envisioned.

Bob was driving, and I was riding shotgun that day when we spied the Dot highway sign.

"Let's drive through," Bob said, "see what's here and turn around at the sign on the other side of town."

Except there was no town — just a convenience store with gas pumps at the intersection with U.S. 421, the road to

Pennington Gap, along with a fruit stand, a construction company, several houses and a few old barns. We drove for two or three miles, and we never saw another sign.

"We must have done something wrong," Bob said.

So, we returned to the original sign and there, on the other side of the same post, we found the second Dot sign. Hello and goodbye, back to back. We laughed. Perfect.

Bob came up with an idea of how he wanted to illustrate the essence of Dot. It required that I find a nearby resident to help us on a subsequent trip. One call led to another and then to Bill Shelburne, a lifelong resident of the community.

"Tell me something about Dot," I said to Shelburne. There was a long pause. "That ought to tell you something," he

said with a laugh.

A farmer and retired school teacher, Shelburne said as far as he knew there was nothing exotic about the origins of the community's name. "Probably because it's a dot on the map," he said.

We met Shelburne at his home, borrowed a 10-foot ladder and drove to the Dot sign in his pickup truck. We gave Shelburne one of those little hand-held mirrors we'd purchased at a nearby store and asked him to stand next to the sign post, while we set up the ladder in the back of his truck. Bob climbed to the top of the ladder, while I stood in the bed of the truck, holding the ladder steady. As traffic whizzed past — wish I could have heard the conversations in those vehicles — the image Bob envisioned came to life: both signs, along with Bill Shelburne, in the same picture.

ABOVE: A white-tailed deer, oblivious to an oncoming car, grazed peacefully beside the Blue Ridge Parkway in October 2007.

RIGHT: In the late afternoon, a hiker walked up a rise near Spy Mountain on the parkway.

OPPOSITE: Autumn leaves and rocks framed a curve near Humpback Rocks on the parkway.

BELOW: The parkway is a favorite destination for motorcyclists.

ABOVE: Fern Heatwole let the world know the Sugar Tree Country Store in McDowell was open for business on a March morning in 2010.

RIGHT: In March 2010 at the end of a harsh winter, a horse stood in a snow-covered field in Highland County.

ABOVE: Horses grazed in a field near Hot Springs in Bath County in October 2010.

LEFT: Falling Spring Falls, just off U.S. 220 between Hot Springs and Covington, presented a postcard-like photo opportunity in October 2010.

BELOW: The Homestead Resort is nestled into the forested countryside in Hot Springs.

ABOVE: An abandoned barn in the Lacey Springs area of Rockingham County, at sunset in July 2007.

RIGHT: A flock of wild turkeys searched for food at the Wachapreague Cemetery on the Eastern Shore in November 2007.

BOTTOM LEFT: The view after sundown from Raven's Roost on the Blue Ridge Parkway in 2007.

BOTTOM RIGHT: In July 2007, a pedestrian ambled past the first structure inside Virginia, an abandoned gas station, about fifty feet from the Virginia–North Carolina line on U.S. 1 in Mecklenburg County.

ABOVE: A cotton field, as the sun set, beside U.S. 13 on the Eastern Shore in November 2007.

LEFT: A field of Brown-Eyed Susans brighten the grounds of the Historic Crab Orchard Museum & Pioneer Park outside Tazewell in 2007.

BELOW: Canada geese headed south past a nearly full moon in the early morning over Varina, east of Richmond.

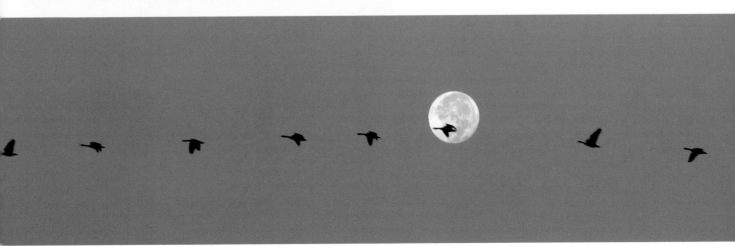

TOP: A young swimmer flipped into the Atlantic surf on Assateague Island near Chincoteague in June 2008.

ABOVE: In November 2010, Dewey Rowland showed off part of the model train layout built by the Lonesome Pine Model Railroaders in the town of Appalachia.

RIGHT: Jeff Holland, executive director of the Chesapeake Bay Bridge-Tunnel, grimaced from the noise of a passing truck inside a tunnel in June 2008. The tunnel connects Virginia Beach to the Eastern Shore of Virginia.

ABOVE: Standing tall against a brooding dawn, the statue of Gen. Thomas J. 'Stonewall' Jackson cut an imposing figure at Manassas National Battlefield Park in July 2007.

LEFT: In October 2009, a Civil War soldier statue appeared to guard workmen repairing the roof of the historic courthouse in Boydton.

TOP: After sunset in September 2007, lights shined in a cabin on the hill above Cuz's Uptown Barbeque in Tazewell County.

ABOVE: The sun sets on the Chesapeake Bay over a fishing pier at Cape Charles, near the southern tip of the Eastern Shore, in November 2007.

ABOVE: In April 2010, Michelle Belton (left), held up the train of the bridal gown of her daughter, Brandy Belton, as photographer Angie Thompson led the way to Mabry Mill on the Blue Ridge Parkway near Meadows of Dan.

LEFT: A family cemetery between mileposts 135 and 136 on the Blue Ridge Parkway.

BELOW: A vintage automobile motored along the parkway near Volunteer Gap.

The Crooked Road

The Crooked Road is the perfect name for the musical heritage trail in Southwest Virginia. Look at a map — or, better yet, hop in your car and see for yourself. It is winding and rambling and almost never straight. The beauty will take your breath away, and the steep grades, mountain-hugging curves and occasional slow-moving coal trucks will summon all the patience you can muster.

Stretching for more than 300 miles between Rocky Mount and Breaks Interstate Park on the Virginia-Kentucky line, the Crooked Road connects small towns and country stores and, through the magic created by fiddles and banjos in the right hands, celebrates the region's Appalachian heritage and history.

Spend a Friday evening at the Floyd Country Store, visit the Carter Family Fold in Hiltons on a Saturday night or catch a concert at the Blue Ridge Music Center. Get up and dance, or just sit and listen. Either works. Drop by one of the regular jams that can be found almost any night of the week in communities all along the road, casual gatherings where the music is remarkably good and the conversation unmistakably authentic.

Music isn't all you'll find. Grayson Highlands State Park, with its hiking trails, magnificent views and wild blueberries, is a treasure. Breaks Park, dubbed "the Grand Canyon of the South" because of its deep river gorge, is no picnic to reach — almost seven hours by car from Richmond — but its rugged beauty is worth the effort. And leave time for towns such as Floyd, Damascus, Abingdon and Big Stone Gap.

Above all, don't be in a hurry. These miles take a while and should. The Crooked Road is not a race to the finish, but a meandering journey with unexpected joys — musical and otherwise — to be discovered along the way.

ABOVE: Trish Kilby (center) was having a great time playing banjo with The Blue Ridge Ramblers as they held an impromptu concert in the campground area of the annual Old Fiddlers' Convention in Galax in August 2002.

ABOVE: New Girls Night Out, an all-women bluegrass band, performed on stage at the Galax fiddlers convention in 2002.

LEFT: Benjamin Ward (left) and Carla Yentzer warmed up for a performance on stage in Galax.

BOTTOM LEFT: Barbara Poole played bass and Larry Sigman old-time clawhammer banjo as a group of fans 'flatfoot' danced in the campground.

BOTTOM RIGHT: Johnny Daniels (on fiddle) and the Pickers Anonymous from Nashville, Tenn., performed on the sidewalk in front of Barr's Fiddle Shop in Galax during the 2002 convention.

LEFT: In 2002, Anne Holton (right), wife of Lt. Gov. Tim Kaine, danced to the music of The Blue Ridge Ramblers at the Galax fiddlers convention.

OPPOSITE TOP: The campground in Galax's Felts Park was packed for the 2002 convention.

OPPOSITE BOTTOM: Pat Ahrens (left) kept rhythm on her 1944 Martin D28 flattop guitar while accompanied by a bass and banjo during an informal jam in the parking lot in Galax.

BELOW: A row of new and old fiddles hung on the wall at Barr's Fiddle Shop.

RIGHT: The music was free at the Star Barber Shop in Bristol, in August 2002, as Charlie Sams sat for a haircut from barber Gene Boyd. The bluegrass pickers who serenaded Sams included (left to right): Dale Mitchell, mandolin; Grady Holman, fiddle; Wilkie Welch, guitar; Gary Wood, bass; Gaines Burke, singing and playing guitar; and Gene Thompson, fiddle.

BELOW: Lori Poteat played electric fiddle with a smile for Celtic Soul, a group from Jacksonville, Fla., during the 2002 Virginia Highlands Festival in Abingdon.

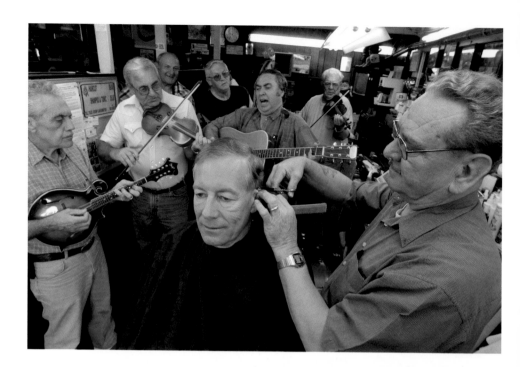

ABOVE: Rita Forrester (center), granddaughter of A. P. Carter, sang "Will the Circle Be Unbroken" with the Cana Ramblers on stage at the Carter Family Fold in Hiltons in July 2010.

LEFT: Forrester reflected on her family history inside the cabin where A.P. Carter was born.

BOTTOM LEFT: Wayne Henderson, who has a long waiting list of musicians who want one of his handcrafted guitars, strummed one of his creations for the first time in his shop in Grayson County in 2005.

BOTTOM RIGHT: A young girl practiced her clogging outside the Carter Family Fold as the Cana Ramblers played on stage.

ABOVE: Patrons reserved seats for the Friday Nite Jamboree at the Floyd Country Store by placing their dancing shoes on the chairs on an April evening in 2010.

RIGHT: Evan Gear (left) of Roanoke, and Jaimie Crandall, of Franklin County, snuggled outside the country store as the music played inside.

ABOVE: Members of the audience danced to the music of Tenbrooks.

RIGHT: Owners Woody and Jackie Crenshaw revived and renovated the Floyd Country Store.

ABOVE: Patrons and musicians crowd into the store and routinely turn downtown Floyd into a bustling place on Friday nights.

LEFT: Serena and Donald Jacobs celebrated after being married on stage during the Friday Nite Jamboree at the Floyd store in April 2010.

ABOVE: Instrument-maker Jack Branch played one of his hand-made fiddles at his home outside Bristol in May 2002 as his wife, Nannie, listened from the doorway.

RIGHT: Paul Kuczko, founder and director of the Lonesome Pine Office on Youth in Big Stone Gap, also started Lonesome Records, a nonprofit organization that records and distributes music from Southwest Virginia to help finance the agency that assists troubled youth and broken families.

BOTTOM LEFT: Iboya Pasley (left) and her husband, Lucas Pasley (right) rehearsed a song as John Perry listened backstage at the Blue Ridge Music Center off the Blue Ridge Parkway near Galax in June 2004.

BOTTOM RIGHT: Eight-year-old James Burcham, of Galax, posed with his guitar and his third-place ribbon that he won at a music festival in Fries in August 2006.

ABOVE LEFT: After hours in the back of Barr's Fiddle Shop in Galax, in 2002, Tyler Reavis, 10, (left), and cousin Houston Caldwell, 10, studied banjo with Steve Barr, whose father owned the shop.

ABOVE RIGHT AND LEFT: In August 2006 at his store in Rocky Mount, Russell Cannaday played the 1933 Gibson RB4 Mastertone banjo, valued at close to $150,000, that belonged to his late father.

BELOW: Country Current, the U.S. Navy's country and bluegrass band, performed in June 2004 at the Blue Ridge Music Center, off the Blue Ridge Parkway near Galax. Band members included (left to right) Pat White, Wayne Taylor, Keith Arneson and Frank Solivan.

Tangier Island

Half the fun of visiting Tangier Island is getting there (the other half is eating your fill of crab cakes or soft-shell crabs).

For most visitors from mainland Virginia (or, as Tangiermen charmingly refer to it, "the western shore") that means catching a seasonal ferry in Reedville and cruising for more than an hour across the Chesapeake Bay.

Others travel by private boat, and I know of at least two guys who paddled a canoe from Reedville across the bay one long ago December and had to pretty much chip the ice off themselves when they arrived on Tangier. They hitched a ride back.

If you are so fortunate, the most efficient way to reach Tangier is by small aircraft that makes use of the island's airstrip. We were privileged to tag along on a few occasions with Dr. David B. Nichols,

a self-described country doctor who also was a pilot with a plane and a helicopter. Once a week for more than 30 years, Nichols flew to Tangier — or sent someone from his White Stone practice — to tend to the medical needs of the island that for many years had no resident physician. He became a trusted friend to the island and its people, who take a while to warm to those from away and are known for their self-reliance, their stubbornness and their old English dialect.

Nichols and his patient and friend Jimmie Carter (who had long since shaken the ice from his wintry canoe paddle to the island) led a fundraising effort to build a much-needed health center for Tangier. Shortly before the center was scheduled to open in 2010, Nichols was diagnosed with inoperable cancer, and the grim news hit the island hard. The turnout for

the dedication of the new center was the very definition of bittersweet, one of the grandest and saddest days the island had ever known. Nichols promised the crowd that day that he would "never leave you in spirit," and he was right. Proving his devotion to the island, he asked that his ashes be buried in the cemetery — next to the David B. Nichols Health Center.

ABOVE: In May 2007, 12-year-old Nathan Crockett jumped from a dock at Tangier Island, an afternoon tradition for the kids of the island.

ABOVE: Dr. David Nichols grew introspective as he showed visitors the island's old health clinic in August 2010. Weeks earlier, Nichols had been diagnosed with inoperable cancer.

LEFT: Most visitors reach Tangier Island by boat, but some fly in and land on the island's airstrip.

BELOW: During the August 2010 dedication of the island's new health center, Nichols waved to the crowd that gathered to show their appreciation to their beloved physician.

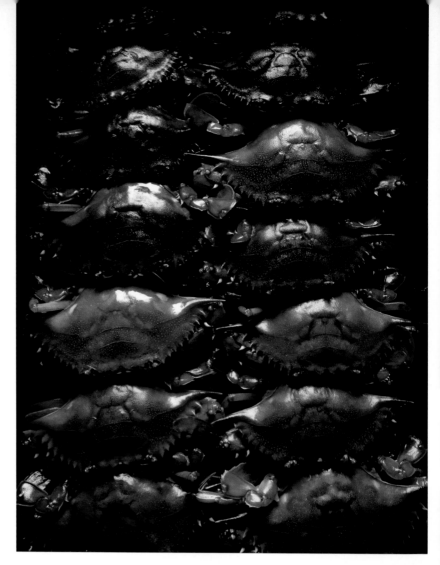

ABOVE: A small American flag fluttered in front of a row of crab pot floats at the island's Rudy Thomas Dock. Each waterman has a unique float color to identify his pots.

RIGHT: A box of soft-shell crabs prepared for shipping off the island.

BELOW: An old boat in the island's repair yard in May 2007.

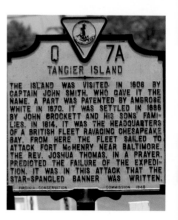

ABOVE: The island is rich in history.

LEFT: Crab pots stacked near the island's dock.

TOP LEFT: A resident pedaled past the island's Double Six Sandwich Shop, a favorite of watermen, on an early morning in June 2007.

MIDDLE LEFT: Carly Marshall, 11, pedaled her twin sister Cassidy along one of the island's roads in May 2007. Motorized vehicles larger than scooters and golf carts are rare on the tiny island.

MIDDLE RIGHT: Bikes clustered in front of the Tangier schoolhouse in May 2007.

BOTTOM: At sunset, Tangier Island seems very alone in the Chesapeake Bay.

Places of Worship

We've sat in pews — and balconies — in churches around Virginia, singing hymns, listening to sermons and finding the most interesting people.

Like the Rev. Edgar J. Burkholder and his wife, Beverly — "Rev and Bev," as it said on their mailbox in Montpelier — who were still preaching and pastoring at Apple Grove Baptist Church in Louisa County in 2009 after 73 years of marriage. He was 94, she 92. "Rev" grew up in a log house in the mountains in Botetourt County and showed us a photo of a hole in the home's front porch, which is where he used to hide as a child whenever the local minister came calling. "I was scared to death of preachers," he said with a laugh. "Still afraid of them."

Like the Rev. Stewart Childress, who left the business world just before turning 50 to enter seminary and follow in

the footsteps of his famous grandfather, the Rev. Robert W. "Bob" Childress, who built a series of lovely little rock churches in rugged communities along the Blue Ridge Parkway. "Stand up, speak up and shut up," Childress said of his preaching philosophy in 2003 when we attended a service at Slate Mountain Church, one of the rock churches where he, like his grandfather, served as pastor. "I try to keep my sermons to 15 minutes. I figure if I can't reach them in that amount of time, I've probably lost them anyway."

Like the Rev. Duane Steele, who on a Saturday afternoon in 2006 led us on a tour of Gladesboro Evangelical Lutheran Church in Southwest Virginia, where he served as pastor for 28 years. "Isn't it gorgeous? I think this is the most beautiful church in Carroll County." Which is saying something since Steele, blind since

birth, had never seen the place. But then, you don't need eyes to recognize beauty.

After the service that Sunday at Gladesboro, we were standing near the back pew talking to Eldon Gardner, who had attended the church for all of his 88 years and had become a close friend of Steele's, driving him to nursing homes to make pastoral visits. We marveled at Steele's longevity at the small, rural church. Gardner joked, "The only reason he's stayed is he couldn't see to leave."

Just then, Steele, whose hearing was perfectly fine, walked past. He overheard the comment, recognized the voice and didn't miss a beat.

"I love you Eldon," he said.

Replied Gardner, "I love you too, Duane."

ABOVE: Held by her mother Rhonda Burnette, 11-month-old Mary Burnette seemed to sing along with the choir in September 2003 at the Slate Mountain Church in Patrick County.

TOP LEFT: The Rev. Stewart Childress delivered a prayer to the congregation of Slate Mountain, one of six stone churches built along the Blue Ridge Parkway by his grandfather, the Rev. Bob Childress.

OPPOSITE: Nine-year-old Jason Jones watched the June 2002 service from the balcony at Mount Calvary Baptist Church in Pleasant Shade.

LEFT: Deaconess Inez Williams (left) whispered to her grandson, Isaac Williams, 4, who was clutching a fan at a Mount Calvary Baptist service in June 2002.

LEFT: The Rev. Duane Steele sang with the choir at the Gladesboro Evangelical Lutheran Church in Gladesboro on a Sunday in August 2006.

OPPOSITE TOP: Bev Burkholder, 92, listened to her husband, the Rev. Edgar J. Burkholder, 94, pastor of the Apple Grove Baptist Church in Mineral during his sermon in December 2009. The day before, the couple celebrated their 73rd wedding anniversary.

OPPOSITE BOTTOM LEFT: An antique car parked at Slate Mountain Church.

OPPOSITE MIDDLE RIGHT: Edgar Burkholder, deep in thought, walked out of his office past a painting of himself performing a ceremony of baptism.

OPPOSITE BOTTOM RIGHT: In the afternoon light, Steele led a detailed tour of his church.

BELOW: At the close of the service, Steele and church member Bobby Willard greeted one another in a moment of levity.

Burke's Garden

"God's Thumbprint" is what they call Burke's Garden, which is precisely what it looks like from above. From ground level, where we experienced it, Burke's Garden is a bowl of lush farmland, ringed by mountains, the highest valley in Virginia at more than 3,000 feet above sea level. It is a place where motorists share the road with local cows (who have the right of way). The camels steer clear of traffic.

The herd of Bactrian (two-hump) camels at Lost World Ranch is just one of the curiosities you'll find in this out-of-the-way pocket of Southwest Virginia. The only paved road into the valley comes over the mountain from the town of Tazewell. The first things you notice upon arriving

in The Garden are signposts bearing the names of local residents along with the distances to their homes. The local phone directory, we discovered on a visit in 2007, was a single sheet of paper.

The Garden gained its name from a 1748 survey team that included a man named James Burke (or Burk), who after a meal buried the peelings of potatoes near a campfire. Subsequent explorers reaching the area discovered a crop of potatoes waiting for them. According to local lore, the Vanderbilts wanted to build a family castle in The Garden in the late 1800s, but were rebuffed by landowners and instead constructed Biltmore in Asheville, N.C.

The Appalachian Trail passes nearby,

so The Garden sees its share of hikers, as well as bicyclists who enjoy pedaling the valley's quiet roads. They just have to keep an eye out for the cows.

ABOVE: Colleen Cox, postmaster for Burke's Garden, stood in the doorway of the tiny post office in August 2007.

LEFT: Nine-year-old Anna Whitted dashed across the pasture as her mom, Charlotte, stared down a large ram protecting the ewes on the family sheep farm, Weatherbury Station.

MIDDLE LEFT: Motorists traveling the valley's roads would do well to keep a wary eye for cows.

MIDDLE RIGHT: A series of detailed signs direct motorists to the homes and farms of Burke's Garden residents.

BOTTOM: A herd of curious young camels gather before an all-terrain vehicle at Lost World Ranch.

County Fairs

What's more American — or Virginian, for that matter — than county fairs? Candy apples and Ferris wheels, tractor pulls and peach preserves, cows and chickens and quilts.

Let's find three very different and very good county fairs, we said in 2003, from different parts of the commonwealth. We asked around and decided on Orange County, an old-fashioned, no-frills, agricultural fair with an emphasis on kids' 4-H projects that at the time was held across the field from James Madison's Montpelier; Russell County, in the mountainous southwest, in what has to be one of the loveliest settings for a fair, or anything, for that matter; and Fairfax County, where the carnival midway and exhibits for the annual Celebrate Fairfax

event were set up in the parking lot of the Fairfax County Government Center.

It was our personal funnel cake tour of Virginia.

As with just about everywhere else we travel, we ran into nothing but nice people, including the Virginia Hams, a jovial barbershop quartet that serenaded us in the shadow of a glass skyscraper in Fairfax, and Russell County landowner Scott White, who overheard Bob asking about possible vantage points for a good picture of the fair and offered a ride in his single-engine plane, taking off and landing at the grass runway of his ranch just down the road.

Then there was 9-year-old Blake Hopkins of Louisa, whom we met on a return visit to the Orange County Fair in

2007. As we walked through a tent of livestock raised by kids, Blake asked if we'd like to make a picture of one of the hogs he brought to show at the fair.

"What's its name?" I asked.

"Olivia!" he responded with great pride.

I suggested that was a pretty nice name for a hog.

With genuine gusto and without even a hint of hesitation, he replied, "That's my girlfriend's name!"

ABOVE: An aerial view (courtesy of a ride from local landowner and pilot Scott White) offered an unparalleled view of the 2003 Russell County Fair.

ABOVE: Second-place winner in the egg category at the Orange County Fair in 2007.

LEFT: Nine-year-old Blake Hopkins of Louisa was extremely proud to show off Olivia, one of the two hogs he brought to show at the Orange County Fair in 2007.

BELOW: Celebrate Fairfax, shown here in 2003, was a different sort of county fair as it was held on the grounds of the Fairfax County government center.

ABOVE: The Virginia Hams — Joe, Wes, Drew and Mike — were only too happy to perform for visitors to Celebrate Fairfax in 2003.

RIGHT: Sophie Passino, 4, (left), of Fluvanna County, went nose-to-nose with Elliott, a goat owned by Meadow Anderson, 5, (right) at the 2007 Orange County Fair.

ABOVE: The old-time clothing worn by 5-year-old Ashley Williams, of Orange County, paired nicely with a handmade quilt at the 2003 Orange County Fair.

LEFT: Best in Show for vegetables at the 2007 Orange County Fair.

BELOW: Ruby Rose and Frisco Slim (Felicity and Matthew Bouvier) performed their "Wild West Follies" before an appreciative audience at the 2007 Orange County Fair.

RIGHT: Always looking for a laugh, Frisco Slim (Matthew Bouvier) paraded around the Orange County fairgrounds.

OPPOSITE TOP: A large crowd gathered to root on the pups in the Jack Russell races at the 2003 Orange County Fair.

OPPOSITE BOTTOM: Schoolchildren, who got out of school early, gave chase during the goat-catching event at the 2003 Russell County Fair near St. Paul.

BOTTOM LEFT: Six-year-old Anna Wiebe, from Fine Felt Farm in Orange County, couldn't have been happier to show off an egg from one of her chickens at the 2003 Orange County Fair.

BOTTOM RIGHT: The piglet outran most of the kids in a contest at the Russell County Fair, but the child who caught it received a blue ribbon — and the piglet.

The Longest Road

Friend and former editor (and bestselling author) Howard Owen suggested U.S. 58, the longest road in Virginia, might be a worthy subject for a series. He didn't have to suggest twice.

For six months in 2002, Bob and I cranked out a story and photo package every Sunday about U.S. 58, beginning in Virginia Beach and winding up in Cumberland Gap — more than 500 miles in length, and around 600 if you include, as we did, Alternate U.S. 58, an off-shoot that loops from Abingdon through Coeburn and Big Stone Gap. When we reached Cumberland Gap we were told we'd started at the wrong end.

It was a marvelous trip, and we met the greatest people everywhere we went. In the far southwest corner of the commonwealth, people seemed genuinely appreciative that someone from Richmond bothered to come see them. It's an

understandable viewpoint, since they live closer to nine state capitals than their own.

On our way from Jonesville to The Gap late one afternoon, we saw a sign for "Old 58" and veered off the new four-lane version for a look. The twisting road took us to an abandoned country store, fronted by an old rusted and leaning Sky Chief gas pump. Bob was shooting a few pictures when a man mowing the grass at the large white house across the road came over to greet us.

His name was Hilton Tunnell, and he told us the store had been operated by his wife's grandparents. That was a while back since Hilton and Winona Tunnell had recently celebrated their 50th wedding anniversary. They raised their children near Knoxville, Tenn. — Hilton was an engineer, Winona a teacher — but had returned to tend to Winona's old home place and to live there part time.

The house, built in the early 1900s, was in an interesting spot: Old 58 ran alongside the house and store; a more modern version of 58, the remnants of which were barely visible, was cut through a ravine directly behind the house; the newest road carried traffic on a bridge visible in the distance.

Bob asked if he could make a picture of the Tunnells, but they were at the end of a long day of cleaning and yard work and didn't feel photogenic. They asked us to stay for dinner, but we needed to get to our destination for the evening: Middleboro, Ky., on the other side of The Gap.

We made a deal: we'd come back for dinner on another trip if they would permit Bob to shoot their photograph. They agreed, and we did.

LEFT: On our return visit in September 2002, Hilton and Winona Tunnell prepared Sunday dinner for us and sat for a photo on the front porch of their home in Lee County.

OPPOSITE: Ashleigh Deemer (left) and friend Katherine Petrie, both from Pittsburgh, Pa., watched the sunrise in May 2002 at the Virginia Beach oceanfront, the eastern terminus of U.S. 58.

BELOW: A highway marker for 'old' U.S. 58 near Hagan in Lee County.

ABOVE: Descendants of Cicero and Rettie Hall gathered at a hilltop cemetery near Volney in August 2002 for a "decoration," an annual event in which families hold reunions and decorate the graves of loved ones.

RIGHT: In June 2002, Chris McCaden (left) and his brother, Mac, provided a tour of their state-of-the-art milking parlor at their dairy farm near Broadnax.

ABOVE: On a Friday night in May 2002, members of the media and fans watched NASCAR-type Grand Stocks line up for the start of their race at the Southampton Motor Speedway in Capron.

RIGHT: Race fans gathered early for the Food City Family Night celebration in August 2002, stepping past the Virginia-Tennessee state line marker in the middle of Bristol's State Street.

BELOW: The Central Drive-in Theatre, between Norton and Appalachia in Southwest Virginia, showed "Star Wars II" on a Friday night in August 2002 as a coal train rumbled slowly behind the screen.

TOP LEFT: Dr. Elizabeth R. Vaughan, also known as the Foxy Doc in part because of pin-up photos such as the one on the hallway wall, checked a patient's file in her Martinsville office in July 2002. On the verge of turning 50, she had completely changed her image from a self-described "overweight nerd" in high school.

TOP RIGHT: Lovers Leap overlook on U.S. 58, near Vesta, in Patrick County.

ABOVE: Visitors to the Pinnacle Overlook at Cumberland Gap — at the end of U.S. 58, where Virginia, Kentucky and Tennessee come together — were treated to a spectacular sunset on a Sunday in September 2002.

Eastern Shore

The wind whipped and the sea roared as we stepped onto Cedar Island, an uninhabited barrier island on the Eastern Shore of Virginia.

The tide had receded, but not for long, and our guide, Rick Kellam, who had steered his 24-foot skiff through two miles of salt marshes to reach the island, told us to move quickly. He warned we had about 30 minutes to look around, gather a few whelk shells and climb back aboard the skiff before the tide returned and covered this slender strip of land — and us.

We hurried along.

Hurricane Noel, or what was left of it, was moving up the East Coast on the second day of November in 2007. The eye of the storm was still out in the Atlantic, but its long-armed fury created an ominous scene: massive waves pounding the beach, and relentless, powerful gusts scattering sand and shorebirds and making it almost impossible for us to hear one another.

"Fantastic!" Kellam hollered over the howl of the wind.

Even the harshest of days on the barrier islands are sheer beauty in the eyes of people like Kellam, who truly love these rare, but fragile pieces of undeveloped and unspoiled earth that probably, he said, look a lot like they did "15 minutes after God created them."

"One of the last great places on Earth left in its natural form and not screwed up by man," he said. "Yet."

The barrier islands and surrounding salt marshes, tidal mudflats and shallow bays that stretch more than 60 miles along the Shore represent the "longest expanse of coastal wilderness remaining on the Eastern Seaboard," according to The Nature Conservancy. The islands are wildlife habitats and among the most important migratory bird stopover and nesting sites on the planet.

"You hear a lot of people say, 'The Eastern Shore of Virginia is like going back in time 50 years,'" said Kellam, who operated an eco-tour company. "My answer to this is, 'And we love every minute of it.'"

Happy Holidays

How do you beat spending Independence Day in Independence? Maybe Valentine's Day in Valentines?

We found ourselves in Independence, the county seat of Grayson County, during our 2002 series on U.S. 58, on the Fourth of July. We watched the homespun parade featuring farm tractors towing floats with little girls dressed as the Statue of Liberty and llamas wearing red, white and blue top hats marching down Main Street. We met the 80-something friends, each dressed in a blue blouse, white slacks and shoes, and star-spangled hats, who showed up early every year with their lawn chairs and claimed their "spots" — prime vantage points in front of the town's

historic courthouse.

In advance of Valentine's Day in 2010, we visited Valentines, a small community in Brunswick County, near the Virginia-North Carolina line. We headed straight for Wright's General Merchandise, a 1930s general store with a squeaky wooden screen door and the community's post office tucked into a corner. As Valentine's Day approaches each year, the cards and letters start trickling into the post office every January and reach flood stage in early February, thousands of pieces of mail from all over the world seeking one thing: the heart-shaped, hand-canceled postmark that says "VALENTINES, VA."

"It's a lot of work," said Postmaster

Kathy Fajna, telling us about the holiday decorations she put up, the school groups and motorcycle clubs that showed up to drop off their mail and the occasional wedding she hosted. Then there are the blisters she would get from postmarking all of that mail by hand.

"It's fun," she said with a laugh, "but I don't know if I could stand it twice a year."

ABOVE: Six-year-old Emily Turner, of Athens, Ga., sat atop a wall on the lawn of the historic courthouse in Independence, a perfect vantage point for the 2002 Fourth of July parade. Emily's mom, Jenny, grew up in Independence.

ABOVE: In January 2010, Valentines postmaster Kathy Fajna sorted mail in the tiny post office and general store where mail arrives from around the world seeking a special postmark for Valentine's Day.

LEFT: Jean Voss, dressed as a Christmas tree, rode Tippy after the Christmas parade in Clifton in December 2004.

BELOW: Tree lights signaled the beginning of the holiday season along King Street in Old Town Alexandria in December 2007.

Pocahontas

Our destination was Pocahontas, an old mining town in the coalfields of Southwest Virginia, nestled in a corner of Tazewell County next to the West Virginia line. In fact, someone mentioned to us we had to drive into West Virginia and then back into Virginia in order to reach Pocahontas.

That was before we noticed a thin gray line on our trusty map that seemed to lead directly to the town without need for going into another state. We're seasoned travelers, right? Experienced navigators? We'd always gotten where we were going, and, more importantly, always gotten home, right? Right?

So, off we went, making a couple of turns, passing a few houses, including one where a woman sat on her porch, and crossing a set of railroad tracks. Then the paved road turned to gravel, and it narrowed as it started making a steep climb around the side of a mountain. Bob made a U-turn in the Ford Focus — not exactly the mountain goat of vehicles — and headed down the mountain.

We came to the woman on her porch, and she said something to the effect, "I wondered when you'd be back."

I explained our predicament and where we were headed. "You can get to Pocahontas the way you were going," she said, "but I wouldn't think you'd want to."

She straightened us out, and we eventually reached Pocahontas, a fading town with a rich history where people from different cultures came to live and work in the heyday of the mines. However, the mines are long closed, the population has dwindled and the one-time thriving company town is crumbling from neglect.

"People have told me the streets would be so full you had to say, 'Excuse me' to pass someone who was walking too slow in front of you," said Mayor Anita Brown, sitting on a bench in front of The Cricket, the town's last restaurant before she closed it the year before our 2007 visit. "I would have loved to have seen it."

ABOVE: On a Sunday afternoon in September 2007, Kelly McDougall, 15, rode past the ruins of the old company store in downtown Pocahontas.

LEFT: Empty jars for embalming fluid sat next to a large family Bible inside the dust-covered shop of William Butts, cabinetmaker, who became a coffin maker and embalmer after the mine disaster in 1884 that killed 114 in Pocahontas.

BELOW: Visitors to the Pocahontas Exhibition Mine, once a working mine and now a tourist attraction, can get a feel for what it was like to work in a mine.

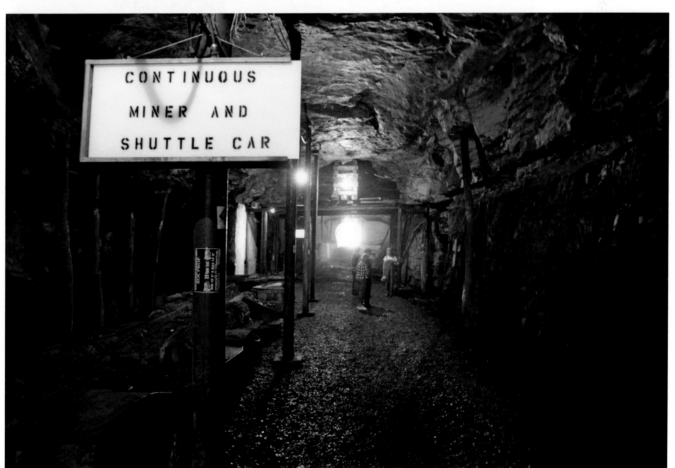

CONTINUOUS MINER AND SHUTTLE CAR

ABOVE: Members of the local American Legion post marched through town as part of the Labor Day parade.

RIGHT: Retired coal miner Billy E. Hylton rode on a flatbed trailer with other retirees being honored on Labor Day.

BELOW: U.S. Rep. Rick Boucher, D-9th, standing on a stump, addressed residents during the 2007 Labor Day festivities.

ABOVE: The sanctuary of St. Elizabeth Catholic Church remains a place of beauty, even as the town crumbles around it.

TOP RIGHT: Three boys tossed a football in a deserted residential street in Pocahontas.

BOTTOM RIGHT: A black cat crossed a downtown street during the 2007 Labor Day festivities in Pocahontas.

School Days

On one of our great days on the road — and there have been many — we were ushered into the gymnasium of the Mt. Rogers Combined School where we found the school band seated in the bleachers and ready to play for us. To be more precise, it was the Albert Hash Memorial Band, which was named for a local fiddling and fiddle-making legend. It featured not tubas and bass drums but fiddles, banjos and mandolins, and it played not Sousa but old-time mountain music. And it sounded wonderful.

The music was but one of the charms of the school in the highlands of Grayson County, at the time in 2002 one of only two public schools in Virginia with K-12 under one roof. (Tangier Combined School, which we've also visited, was the other.) We also were introduced to members of that year's Mt. Rogers senior class:

all seven of them.

The original 1930s stone schoolhouse, on a bend in one of the most coiled sections of U.S. 58, had been expanded over the years to accommodate more students. By the time we visited, technology linked students by computers and television monitors to other schools so they could study academic subjects not offered at a school with only 98 students and 14 faculty members. Technology didn't affect everything, though. The school's "intercom" was pretty much, as one teacher put it, "Holler down the hall!"

All that's changed now. We returned to Mt. Rogers in the fall of 2010 after a new school opened a dozen miles down the mountain with modern amenities, including an actual intercom system. The old place was ghostly quiet as Emily Spencer, the school's longtime music teacher,

showed us around one last time. When we reached the gym, we asked Emily if she would play a tune on her banjo for a video we were putting together.

As we sat transfixed, she flawlessly performed a hauntingly beautiful version of "House Carpenter."

"Was that all right?" she asked when she was finished.

Perfect.

ABOVE: Seven-year-old Amber Bradley, illuminated by the early morning light, sat in her seat on Craig County school bus No. 15 in September 2004, watching the farmland roll by after she and her 9-year-old sister Jennifer were the first students picked up on a bus that made a 42-mile loop each morning and afternoon.

ABOVE: Amber and Jennifer Bradley waited for the bus outside their home in Craig County.

LEFT: The Edwards family — Trevor, 2nd grade, Emmalee, 4th grade, Lara, 9th grade and Jessica , 10th grade — bounded from their home to board bus No. 15.

BELOW: Dylan Frango, a talkative 2nd-grader with a mischievous grin, didn't seem to mind the long ride to school.

ABOVE: The Peters Brothers — (left to right) Arthur Peters, Fleming Partin and Tollie Fleming — were the house band at the historic Tacoma School in the town of Tacoma. They warmed up before their performance on a Saturday evening In September 2002. The community held a dance and cakewalk each Saturday to raise money to restore the old schoolhouse.

RIGHT: Under gathering storm clouds, a Confederate flag flew over the Corinth Baptist Church Cemetery in Ben Hur, while across U.S. 58 fans filed into the Lee High School stadium for a Lee-Gate City football game in September 2002.

ABOVE: Emily Spencer, long-time music teacher at the Mt. Rogers Combined School in Grayson County, talked about the school's 2010 (and last) graduating class, which included three students.

LEFT: Spencer served as director of the school's Albert Hash Memorial Band, which gathered in the gym to perform in August 2002.

BELOW: Eight years later, in July 2010, Spencer sat alone in the same gym, Mt. Rogers having been closed after construction of a new school.

The Valley Road

We spent the summer of 2013 traveling U.S. 11, one of the oldest roads in America, and we found much history, many charming towns and timeless beauty. Also potato chips and dinosaurs.

In Virginia, the old highway stretches between Bristol and just north of Winchester. It follows a trail blazed by Native American warriors and pioneers, Civil War soldiers and long-haul truckers. It parallels Interstate 81, which was constructed in the 1960s. The modern highway took much of the traffic from U.S. 11, forcing some businesses to close, but the old road didn't dry up. There is much to see and do along U.S. 11, and, if you have the time, it remains a far more pleasant, civilized way to travel through the valley of Virginia.

On our 300-mile journey along U.S. 11 in Virginia, we found a place called Rest, apple blossoms in Winchester and assorted bridges: Natural Bridge, a swinging bridge in Buchanan and a covered bridge on the way to the Route 11 Potato Chips factory. We discovered Shakespeare in Staunton, frontier log cabins, gloriously restored movie houses and old train depots, a rooftop garden in Roanoke, Civil War battlefields, lots of colleges and universities, Asian pears, legal moonshine, music jams and in Bristol a giant guitar, just before the road disappeared into Tennessee and beyond.

It's difficult to fathom another road providing a more thorough representation of Virginia.

Among our stops was Enchanted Castle Studios, Mark Cline's wacky laboratory, a madly mirthful place on the side of U.S. 11, between Lexington and Natural Bridge. Cline sculpts giant monsters, insects and dinosaurs, as well as an occasional Elvis. He's the man behind Foamhenge, the plastic foam reproduction of Stonehenge that can be found on a hill just south of his studio, and numerous other creations along the road, including a statue of Stonewall Jackson near Devils Backbone Brewery in Lexington.

"Route 11," he said, "has presented itself as a canvas to me. "I make good use of that route."

And so did we.

ABOVE: Artist Mark Cline is known for his imaginative creations, such as the full-sized Tyrannosaurus Rex that lives outside his workshop near Natural Bridge.

LEFT: Jim Stroop (left) and Donald Bowers, lifelong residents of New Market, sat outside Simple Tymes antiques shop on a May evening in 2013, chatting and watching the traffic go through town on U.S. 11.

BELOW: The Meem's Bottom Covered Bridge, just off U.S. 11 near Mount Jackson, remains busy with traffic.

ABOVE: Sarah Cohen, founder of Route 11 Potato Chips, started her company at an old feed store in Middletown, before moving the factory to a larger facility near Mount Jackson.

RIGHT: Shooter Brown (left) and Herman Barrett found common ground in bluegrass music at the weekly Smyth County Jam in Chilhowie.

FAR RIGHT: A road sign on Main Street — U.S. 11 — in Lexington

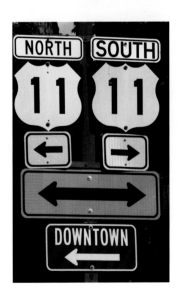

ABOVE: A swinging pedestrian bridge — built on stone piers dating to the 1850s — parallels the U.S. 11 vehicle bridge that crosses the James River at Buchanan.

RIGHT: Virginia Sweetwater Moonshine, produced in Marion and sold in liquor stores around Virginia, is that rarest form of mountain moonshine: legal.

BELOW: Tap room manager Brittany Crandall poured handcrafted beer at the Devils Backbone Outpost Brewery on U.S. 11 outside Lexington.

ABOVE: Sitting in a replica of his ancestors' original cabin and surrounded by fleece from his freshly shorn sheep, Lewis Ingles (Bud) Jeffries, the seventh generation of his family to live at Ingles Farm in Radford, talked about the nearby ferry that carried travelers on the Great Wagon Road across the New River.

LEFT: American Shakespeare Center co-founders Jim Warren (left) and Ralph Alan Cohen on stage at Staunton's Blackfriars Playhouse, the world's only re-creation of Shakespeare's original indoor theater.

BELOW: The Pink Cadillac Diner near Natural Bridge.

Chiles Cridlin (left) and Daven Lucy stirred Brunswick stew as the dawn's early light in October 2004 streamed into the Lawrenceville Volunteer Fire Department in Lawrenceville.

FOOD

Potluck

We spent a night in the fire station in Lawrenceville, stirring a vat of Brunswick stew with a paddle, and we helped cheese-making nuns at a monastery in Crozet make a batch of Gouda. In other words, not only will we go anywhere for food, we also are quite willing to work for it.

Traveling around Virginia offers an abundance of opportunities to sample locally produced food and drink and try down-home specialties. We enjoy just about all food and are more than happy to try anything once. I'm thinking of our breakfast at the Hillsville Diner — a place we love — that included a stack of pancakes smothered in sausage gravy with scrambled eggs on the side. We like all of those things, just not necessarily touching each other. But we cleaned our plate. Then there was the joint where everything on the menu seemed to be fried except the

sweet tea, and we weren't sure about that. Again, we cleaned our plate.

When it comes to food, we are flexible.

We've reported on the making of fruitcakes and potato chips, visited wineries, breweries and cideries — and sampled all of the products. Lest you think we ignore healthy stuff, we have made numerous stops at farmers' markets and roadside vegetable stands. You can't beat cantaloupes from Halifax County or sweet potatoes from the Eastern Shore or fresh produce from just about anywhere around the commonwealth.

We've gone into the woods of Highland County with syrup-makers to tap old sugar maples and watched the cold, clear liquid trickle out one drop at a time. We've visited modern sugar camps where giant evaporators turn out syrup as well as an old-fashion sugar house where the sugar

water is collected in buckets and then, over wood fires, cooked in a broad, open pan and in a cast-iron kettle. Tim Duff took a break from stirring and poured us each a small glass of warm syrup. Can't say I've tasted anything better.

We have experienced a remarkable number of serendipitous days on the road.

While in Bristol, we went to see instrument-maker Jack Branch and his wife, Nannie, to talk about fiddles and wound up spending the afternoon at their kitchen table. Jack pulled a ham from the rafters of their curing shed, Nannie made biscuits in a skillet and they poured us glasses of their homemade muscadine wine. It was, as you might suspect, a good afternoon.

ABOVE: Breakfast cooks on the grill at the Hillsville Diner.

OPPOSITE: C. D. 'Mac' McPeak delivered a plate of hotcakes with eggs at his Hillsville Diner in July 2002. McPeak said he arrives at work shortly after 2 a.m. to start frying bacon and making other preparations for the day.

TOP RIGHT: Pancakes and hometown maple syrup were staples at High's Restaurant in Monterey in March 2010.

MIDDLE RIGHT: Cider is produced at several places around Virginia, including Albemarle Cider Works in North Garden.

BOTTOM RIGHT: Crab cakes, such as this plate full that didn't last long at a September 2009 lunch at Hilda Crockett's Chesapeake House, are a specialty on Tangier Island.

BELOW: Waitress Misty France served breakfast and worked the cash register at the Hillsville Diner in July 2002.

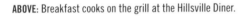

ABOVE: In October 2008, Robbin Smith, owner and chef of The Chesapeake in Cape Charles, prepared shrimp and grits, a favorite of then-presidential candidate Barack Obama. The dish was part of a Cape Charles restaurant promotion highlighting the 2008 election between Obama and John McCain.

RIGHT: A glass of fresh, warm maple syrup, made the old-fashioned way by Tim Duff at his sugar house in Highland County in March 2010, hit the spot.

BELOW: Making maple syrup the old-fashioned way, Tim Duff skimmed the boiling syrup water from the pan at his sugar house in Highland County in March 2010.

ABOVE: Breakfast was as good as it looked at the Cape Charles House Bed & Breakfast in November 2007.

LEFT: Mattie Clayton was still making fruitcakes at age 90 in December 2008 at her daughter's County Seat Restaurant in Powhatan.

BOTTOM LEFT: Calvin Myers, owner of Caloman's Kitchen in Orange, was busily cooking at the 2007 Orange County Fair.

BOTTOM MIDDLE: Breakfast was served in August 2002 at the Mountain Laurel Inn, a bed-and-breakfast in Damascus.

BOTTOM RIGHT: Tailgating outside Rogers Stadium before a football game at Virginia State University in October 2003, a group of friends — (left to right) Russell Jenkins, Lester Lawrence and Mike East — enjoyed a laugh while waiting for breakfast to finish cooking. After breakfast, they planned to eat lunch and then attend the game.

RIGHT: Doug Flemer, owner of Ingleside Vineyards in Oak Grove, the oldest winery on Virginia's Northern Neck, poured a glass for tasting after leading a tour in September 2008.

MIDDLE LEFT: Villa Appalaccia, a winery on the Blue Ridge Parkway, produces a number of wines, including Sangiovese.

MIDDLE RIGHT: In May 2002, kegs of wine were stacked floor to ceiling at Chateau Morrisette, a winery just off the Blue Ridge Parkway near Meadows of Dan.

BOTTOM LEFT: Thomas Jefferson was a noted wine connoisseur, though he had little luck growing grapes.

BOTTOM RIGHT: Owner Jon Wehner shared a taste of one of his prize-winning wines at Chatham Vineyards in Machipongo, on Virginia's Eastern Shore in June 2008.

TOP: Marge Beville, owner of the Nottoway Restaurant in Brunswick County in August 2009. Her grandparents started the restaurant on U.S. 1 in 1929, and it became a destination for down-home cooking and some of the best rolls anywhere.

MIDDLE LEFT: The hands of Sister Barbara held a two-pound wheel of the Gouda cheese produced in 2011 by the nuns at Our Lady of the Angels Monastery in Crozet.

MIDDLE RIGHT: In May 2012, a diner dug into a hot roast beef sandwich and mashed potatoes at the Cumberland Restaurant in Cumberland.

LEFT: The shelves of Poor Farmer's Market in Meadows of Dan, just off the Blue Ridge Parkway, are full of interesting items.

ABOVE: Apple pie a la mode at Kathy's Restaurant in Staunton.

TOP RIGHT: Ellen Anderson (left), the 88-year-old mother of restaurant owner Kathy Lacey, made and delivered the apple pies to Kathy's Restaurant in Staunton on a June day in 2013.

BOTTOM RIGHT: Specialty of the house: cherry pie with ice cream at the Mount Vernon Inn Restaurant at George Washington's Mount Vernon in November 2007.

BOTTOM LEFT: In August 2002, Willie Kilgore, mother of Virginia Attorney General Jerry Kilgore (right) and his twin brother, Del. Terry Kilgore, R-Gate City, served visitors a plate of fried apple pies in the kitchen of the family home outside Gate City.

YOUNG ADVENTURER

ABOVE: Coconut cream pie at the Lakeview Restaurant in Fancy Gap.

LEFT: Nannie Branch of Bristol, posed with her biscuits, just before they disappeared in August 2002.

BELOW: Nannie's husband, Jack Branch, fiddler and fiddle-maker, sipped a cup of coffee in May 2002. He shared a jug of his homemade Muscadine wine with visitors.

At the Table

We've eaten in some interesting places on our road trips: a slow-moving train on the Eastern Shore, a destination restaurant in tiny Chilhowie where nationally regarded chefs prepared multicourse meals that looked almost too pretty to eat, a drive-in near Pennington Gap where customers were encouraged to toss their trash on the parking lot and a barbecue trailer parked at the traffic circle in Chincoteague. I'm not sure the mess hall at Virginia Military Institute counts.

But Cuz's, which defies easy description, surely does. We found out about Cuz's Uptown Barbeque the same way we find out about a lot of places: someone, bless their heart, told us about it.

In the case of Cuz's, we were headed to Burke's Garden, a lovely valley in the mountains of Tazewell County. Charlotte Whitted, executive director of Tazewell's Historic Crab Orchard Museum and Pioneer Park and a resident of Burke's Garden, mentioned we really ought to eat dinner at Cuz's.

It doesn't look like much from the outside, she said, and it might even seem a bit off-putting, but it's well worth the stop. She was right.

Driving along U.S. 460 near the community of Pounding Mill, we came upon an old dairy barn painted hot pink. The weather vane atop the barn's tin roof looked like a pig. It was. The wooden fence around the place bore what appeared to be graffiti, but was extremely intentional art.

Cuz's was a different sort of place inside, too, the walls covered with brightly colored murals, and each hand-painted booth reflecting some sort of outlandish theme. A collection of superhero figures dangled from a door frame. A Richard Nixon mask hung from a wine rack, just above the cabernet sauvignon. The place exuded fun, and the food — fresh, homemade and including a little bit of everything — was terrific.

Mike and Yvonne Thompson opened the place in the late 1970s, converting an idle barn on Mike's family farm into

a tiny restaurant. It was a leap of something beyond faith for Mike, an art history major with a wicked sense of humor, and Yvonne, a Hong Kong-born journalist who came to Southwest Virginia for a newspaper job straight out of college. You might say they've done all right. They have developed a loyal following (near and far), survived a couple of fires and are successful enough they can close during the winter. The place has become an institution.

"The food is the kind of food I would like to eat," Mike said, explaining their approach. "It's simple food, simply cooked."

ABOVE: Sixteen-year-old Robin Adkins (left) and her friend, Lizzie Pack, 87, ate lunch at the Hilltop Cyber Cafe in Vesta, on U.S. 58, in May 2002.

LEFT: In September 2007, owners Yvonne and Mike Thompson greeted diners inside Cuz's Uptown Barbeque a gourmet restaurant just outside Pounding Mill on U.S. 460 in Tazewell County.

MIDDLE LEFT: Woody's Beach BBQ was a popular stop in June 2008 at the traffic circle in Chincoteague.

MIDDLE RIGHT: Lunch at Allman's Bar-B-Q, on U.S. 1 in Fredericksburg, was a plate of pulled pork with hush puppies and cole slaw in August 2009.

BOTTOM LEFT: It doesn't look much like a restaurant, but Cuz's, housed in a former barn, is a good one.

BOTTOM RIGHT: Mary Elizabeth Brown, 76, known at Allman's as "Mom," joked with visitors in August 2009, but still wouldn't reveal the secret recipe of her barbecue sauce.

ABOVE: The meatloaf special with mashed potatoes and butterbeans was lunch in June 2013 at Kathy's Restaurant in Staunton.

RIGHT: Breakfast home fries spilled over the edge of the plate at the Blue Ridge Restaurant in Floyd in April 2010.

BELOW: Prime rib coming out of the oven at Cuz's Uptown Barbeque.

ABOVE: Crab cakes were on the menu in the Bay Creek Railway's dining car, where a four-course dinner was served in June 2008 while the self-propelled rail car ran from Cape Charles to Cheriton and back.

LEFT: A patron of the Patio Drive-In, outside Pennington Gap, was merely following tradition when she tossed her lunch trash out of the car into the parking lot of the restaurant in September 2002. The parking lot was cleaned nightly.

BELOW: Mary and Joseph Daniel (center), of Norfolk, celebrated their 57th wedding anniversary with dinner aboard The Bay Creek Railway. At right is engineer Alex Parry.

ABOVE: Wine pairings were part of the appeal at the Town House, an upscale restaurant in Chilhowie.

RIGHT: The shrimp cocktail arrived looking like a work of art at the Historic Eastville Inn in June 2008.

BELOW: In the kitchen of the Town House in Chilhowie, Karen Urie Shields (right) painstakingly worked on a dessert as (left to right), her husband, John B. Shields, Ben Hester and Edwin Bloodworth hovered over the main course in July 2010. The Town House attracted diners who drove hundreds of miles for a meal.

ABOVE: Chilled vegetable 'minestrone' at the Town House in Chilhowie.

LEFT: At the Horseshoe Restaurant in South Hill, Lynne Ezell brought out the chicken liver and fried chicken dinners as owner Doug Smith looked on in June 2002.

Food Festivals

On the ride home from the 2002 Virginia Pork Festival in Emporia, we started tallying up the different variations of pork we'd sampled that day.

Ham biscuits, barbecued loin chops, Italian sausage, country fried ham and red eye gravy, BLTs, pork fried rice, bologna steak burgers, barbecued Boston butt, even chitterlings. Suddenly, we didn't feel so good. Then I remembered chatting with a volunteer before the gates opened at the Greensville Ruritan Club Grounds as we discussed what would be available at the festival at which tons and tons of pork are prepared in just about every way you can imagine and a few you probably can't.

"Everything on the pig," the volunteer said, "except the oink."

On that trip we also attended the Virginia Cantaloupe Festival in South Boston, where we ate a little of everything, including cantaloupes the size of bowling balls — with vanilla ice cream filling the scooped-out centers. A few years later, we found our way to Whitetop Mountain in Grayson County for the annual ramp festival. A highlight was the ramp-eating contest. Participants raced against the clock and their own judgment to see how many raw ramps — wild leeks that grow in the mountains of Appalachia — they could devour in three minutes. First prize in adult competition was $100 and a big bottle of Scope.

On one of our first road-trip assignments, in the summer of 1993, editors sent us to several of the food festivals around Virginia and wanted us to chronicle the way food and politics mix at the events during campaign season. That was the year Republican George F. Allen and Democrat Mary Sue Terry were running for governor. It was a little like sending pyromaniacs to cover a fire.

We visited the Virginia Chicken Festival in Crewe, and the Eastern Shore of Virginia Seafood Festival in Chincoteague. For the Shad Planking in Wakefield, we arrived in the middle of the night to watch bleary-eyed volunteers ignite the fires that would dance wildly in the pre-dawn darkness and then settle down to slowly smoke the bony fish that had been nailed to wooden planks. As something of a reward for being up so early, we were treated to a breakfast of eggs and shad roe at dawn. We were living large and feeling fine until we remembered it would be hours before the shad would be properly cooked and the politicians would arrive.

ABOVE: In March 2010, Fern Heatwole walked past the potbelly stove on a cold morning at the Sugar Tree Country Store in McDowell, in Highland County, home of the annual Highland Maple Festival.

ABOVE: Getting into the spirit of things, Jim Register (left), of Emerald Island, N.C., and Bob Foster, of Raleigh, N.C., were properly attired with pig snouts as they entered the 2002 Virginia Pork Festival in Emporia.

LEFT: A planked shad at the 63rd annual Shad Planking in Wakefield in April 2011.

BOTTOM LEFT: Jill Elliott, a visitor from Atlanta, tried the ice cream in a cantaloupe at the 2002 Virginia Cantaloupe Festival in South Boston.

BOTTOM RIGHT: Carl Nyman threw another oak log on the fire at the 2011 Shad Planking.

RIGHT: Joyce and Ronnie Greene, owners of Poor Farmer's Farm in Vesta, talked about the upcoming 2002 cabbage festival they would host at their farm.

BOTTOM LEFT: The chicken dinner included fresh ramps — members of the onion family that grow in the mountains of Appalachia — at the Whitetop Mountain Ramp Festival in May 2005.

BOTTOM RIGHT: Jody Davis won first place in the ramp-eating contest, devouring 50 ramps in three minutes.

OPPOSITE TOP: Twelve-year-old John Wayne McCready (left) ate his way to second place and Colten Hess, 12, won first prize in the youth division of the ramp-eating contest.

OPPOSITE BOTTOM LEFT: As the music played, a plate of ramps awaited contestants in the ramp-eating contest.

OPPOSITE BOTTOM RIGHT: Winners of the ramp-eating contest won cash prizes as well as bottles of mouthwash.

Acknowledgments

It would be impossible in this limited space to properly thank everyone who has helped bring this book to fruition: the strangers who befriend us on the road with hospitality and directions, the editors who give us the freedom to roam the state and chase these stories, the colleagues who give us a hard time when we report about the double-scoop of ice cream we eat for lunch while gallivanting around the countryside, the readers who encourage us to do more.

We want to offer a special thanks to our friend Tim Timberlake — familiar radio voice, talented musician and photographer, seasoned traveler, nice guy — who wrote the generous foreword, graciously resisting the urge to tell the truth.

Most of all, we'd like to thank our families, who provide unconditional love, support and patience, as well as occasional editing suggestions, and have never (so far) given in to the temptation to change the locks while we're out of town.

Bill Lohmann and Bob Brown
August 2013